SIGNIFICANT SEED

---✿---

PERPETUAL HARVEST

RICK THOMAS

SIGNIFICANT SEED – PERPETUAL HARVEST
Copyright © 2005 by Rick Thomas

ISBN: 0-9740880-6-4

Published by

LifeBridge
Books
P.O. BOX 49428
CHARLOTTE, NC 28277

Printed in the United States of America.

DEDICATION

To my Covenant Partner, my wife Kathy:
Who has challenged me to pursue
God's destiny for my life in all things;
to never settle for less and always
believe God for the best.

Contents

INTRODUCTION

When the Holy Spirit instructed me to write this book, I was very excited about the project because I have spent my entire life and ministry preaching and practicing what you are about to read.

Sowing seed was something I was very familiar with, even as a child. My parents, both ministers themselves, set the standards of tithing, sowing and reaping within our home and hearts at the very beginning of our lives. We were *givers*—and valued our tithe and offerings greatly since we knew we were being obedient to God.

What we didn't understand was the *significance* of the harvest these gifts would produce if we "expected" the harvest to occur. It is because of this great lesson that I feel this book will revolutionize your thinking on tithes, offerings and gifts.

Here is the number one principle God taught me concerning sowing:

The sowing of a seed gives <u>recognition</u> to a <u>harvest</u> which has not yet been <u>revealed</u> to the <u>senses,</u> but has been <u>mandated</u> by the law of the <u>Spirit.</u>

I also learned that a seed of significance has to be *meaningful*, have *value*, and be of *importance*.

As you will discover on these pages, your **Seed of Significance**:

- Should represent a defining moment.
- Should clarify the passion of your heart.
- Should draw on the gifts of greatness within you.
- Should set in motion a clear path toward your God-given destiny.
- Should establish the type of harvest you are looking for.
- Should demonstrate your faith in God and His Word to do the impossible.
- Should be a clear statement of faith (1) that you will no longer be held captive by your circumstances and (2) that fear, doubt and unbelief have lost their ability to control your life!

The sowing of Seeds of Significance makes for an atmosphere of reproduction with purpose and value. So great is the outcome, it:

- Creates joy, peace and contentment.
- Brings success for yourself with God and others.
- Results in prosperity and strength.
- Produces a secure life!

My friend, this book was written with you, your family and your purpose and destiny in mind. I want you to have all God has provided so you may fulfill *everything* He desires for your future.

I believe by learning to sow significant seeds you not only see your dreams, desires and assignments come to fruition you will reap a *perpetual* harvest.

May God bless you as you begin this journey. I am praying it will transform your life into one of continual blessing.

– Rick Thomas

CHAPTER 1

THE DIVINE PRINCIPLE

What I am about to share is not a man made, self-help formula for personal success. If that were true, we could instantly transform the world from poverty to prosperity in five easy steps.

The roots of sowing a significant seed which produces a perpetual harvest began long before God delivered His law to Moses on Mount Sinai. It can be traced to the beginning of time—when the Almighty created man.

The Bible tells us, *"the Lord God formed the man from the dust of the ground and breathed into his nostrils the breath of life, and the man became a living being"* (Genesis 2:7).

What an incredible miracle! God actually took the clay of the earth, transformed it into the shape of a human being and sowed His breath into Adam.

This began a never-ending cycle of giving and

11

receiving that exists to this very day and will last throughout eternity.

What an amazing process. In order to receive another breath, we must be willing to give up the one we have. And, as we will see, it is impossible to walk in the abundance of God if you try to hold onto the first blessing He ever gave you!

Every breath you take is only possible because you are willing to give up what you already possess.

If you refuse, what you have will immediately become stale, and you will be ineffective and powerless!

Breathing and exhaling, giving and receiving, sowing and reaping—these are divine principles established at the foundation of the world.

The Father's Promise

Because of man's disobedience, God destroyed the earth with a great flood. Only Noah, his family and the animals he sheltered in the ark were saved to repopulate the world once more.

Then the Lord gave two important promises to

Noah. The first was a rainbow as a sign of covenant; then God made this statement, *"As long as the earth endures, seedtime and harvest, cold and heat, summer and winter, day and night will never cease"* (Genesis 8:22).

This divine principle is still at work.

Back to the Basics

Recently, I was speaking at a conference and was shocked when some people told me, "We don't preach tithing in our church."

"Why not?" I wanted to know. "What *do* you preach?"

"Oh," they replied, "tithing was under the law. It's not meant for today. So, we preach seedtime and harvest."

"Well," I responded, "you mean *tithing* then?"

Once again they insisted, "No, tithing is under the law." Opening the Bible to Malachi where God speaks concerning bringing the tithe into the storehouse, politely, I told them they needed to go back much earlier in Scripture—prior to the law—to what was instituted.

God's Portion

The first children on earth, Cain and Abel, offered a portion of their income to the Lord. The Bible records, *"Abel kept flocks, and Cain worked the soil. In the course of time Cain brought some of the fruits of the soil as an offering to the Lord. But Abel brought fat portions from some of the firstborn of his flock. The Lord looked with favor on Abel and his offering"* (Genesis 4:2-4).

Long before the time of Moses God spoke to Abram (before the Lord changed his name to Abraham, the father of many nations), that *"all the peoples of the earth will be blessed through you"* (Genesis 12:3). Then after a great victory, the high priest, Melchizedek, blessed Abram, saying, *"'Blessed be Abram by God Most High, Creator of heaven and earth. And blessed be God Most High, who delivered your enemies into your hand.' Then Abram gave him a tenth of everything"* (Genesis 14:19-20).

And let's not forget about Jacob. After the Lord gave him a dream at Bethel, he made a vow, saying, *"If God will be with me and will watch over me on this journey...this stone that I have set up as a pillar will be God's house, and of all that you give me I will give you a tenth"* (Genesis 28:20,22).

It is clear that tithing was established long before the law was written.

Why is this so important? We need to fully grasp that seedtime and harvest—and tithing—are not under the law, but are principles basic to our relationship with God.

The Ten Commandments were given as laws for the children of Israel to live by—to give them direction and to be a "school master" over them until the day God would send His Son to be our Messiah.

The Glorious Exchange

You see, when you release your substance—your talent, ability or that which you have earned with your efforts—you are releasing a part of your life.

So when you freely offer a ministry your finances, time or prayer, you are declaring "God is my source. He is the Most High God, the possessor of heaven and earth. My trust is not in what I have, but it is in the Creator of the substance!"

More than once I've been asked, "Pastor, should we believe for God to bless us when we give?"

Such people belong to the "Bless Me Club"—I'll bless You if You bless me.

No, you must sow and give based on an understanding of who God is. The Father states, "Because you have given to declare who I am, Now I am going to bless you because of who you are!"

As children of the Most High God, the Lord says, "When the seed that is in your hand is released into My kingdom, then I take the blessing that is in my hand and release it into your life. When you turn loose of your seed, I will turn loose of my harvest!"

What a glorious exchange!

This is a principal of truth God has instituted for *all* believers.

"Running Over"

Jesus says, *"Give, and it will be given to you. A good measure, pressed down, shaken together and running over, will be poured into your lap. For with the measure you use, it will be measured to you"* (Luke 6:38).

In today's language, the larger your scoop, the bigger your blessing. The Lord is talking about *significant* seed producing an incredible "running-over" return.

I cannot overemphasize this truth. The secret to bountiful receiving is to give based on declaring who God is—not because you are "giving to get." The Lord knows your heart and says, "Because you've made known who I am, Now I am going to declare who *you* are and am pouring out a harvest into your life!"

Givers and Takers

There are two kinds of people in this world—givers and takers.

A giver is a supplier.
A taker is a user.

A giver constantly searches after success and
    prosperity for everyone and everything
    around him.
A taker constantly attempts to devalue everyone
    and everything around him.

A giver gives when times are both good and bad.
A taker takes when times are good (because it
    may get worse) and bad (because he is afraid
    he may never have the chance again).

A giver gives as a lifestyle to prosper all he
    meets.
A taker's lifestyle is to take and keep from all he
    comes in contact with.

When you understand God's divine principle of
seedtime and harvest, giving will become as natural
as breathing. And, oh, it will feel so good!

CHAPTER 2

YOUR ULTIMATE SOURCE!

In a recent conversation a fellow minister told me, "We just can't seem to find the secret of getting people to understand our burden and need so they will sow into our ministry."

I asked him, "Do you talk about God blessing them for the seed they sow?"

"Of course not," he quickly responded, "I don't want to manipulate them!"

Rather than argue, I asked the gentleman if he believed his work was of God. "Yes, of course," he replied. Then I wanted to know if he felt a divine calling into that ministry. Again, the answer was a definite "Yes."

"Then you're not manipulating people," I assured him, "you are declaring a truth." And I added, "By having people give to the Lord's work without expecting Him to bless them is robbing these individuals of the blessing God intended."

When believers invest their time, talent and treasure into God's Kingdom for the right reasons, of course they will receive a return!

Some people place their money in a savings account and argue with the bank over the low interest rate—looking for all they can get.

You may say, "But the bank is not God."

That's true. The Lord gives a *much higher* return than you'll ever receive from any earthly financial institution!

The Results of Faithfulness

I trust you realize your Heavenly Father desires you be successful in every way—spiritually, physically and financially.

Listen to these words written by John the apostle to his Christian friend Gaius, *"Beloved, I wish above all things that thou mayest prosper and be in health, even as thy soul prospereth"* (3 John 1:2 KJV).

Without question, this is a powerful verse. Yet if you continue to read John's letter, you will understand its full significance. He writes, *"It gave me great joy to have some brothers come and tell about your faithfulness to the truth and how you continue to walk in the truth. I have no greater joy than to hear that my children are walking in the truth"* (vv.3-4).

Faithfulness brings God's blessing. As the apostle Paul told the believers at Galatia, *"And let us not be weary in well doing: for in due season we shall reap, if we faint not"* (Galatians 6:9 KJV).

In John's letter, he commends Gaius, a servant of the Lord, for walking in truth—this man had the Word within him. And he added, *"Dear friend, you are faithful in what you are doing for the brothers, even though they are strangers to you"* (3 John 1:5).

It was the man's obedience to the Word and the fact that he sowed into the lives of others which resulted in a blessing of total prosperity.

John was saying, "Gaius, I've heard how you've taken care of your friends and given of your substance, therefore, you have a right to expect God to bless you."

What a perfect role model for us.

The Giver's Reward

One of my favorite chapters in the New Testament

is Philippians 4. The apostle Paul encourages us to:

- **Rejoice.** *"Rejoice in the Lord always. I will say it again: Rejoice!"* (Philippians 4:4).
- **Be gentle.** *"Let your gentleness be evident to all. The Lord is near"* (v.5).
- **Be thankful.** *"Do not be anxious about anything, but in everything, by prayer and petition, with thanksgiving, present your requests to God"* (v.6).
- **Let God's peace protect you.** *"And the peace of God, which transcends all understanding, will guard your hearts and your minds in Christ Jesus"* (v.7).
- **Think the right thoughts.** *"Finally, brethren, whatsoever things are true, whatsoever things are honest, whatsoever things are just, whatsoever things are pure, whatsoever things are lovely, whatsoever things are of good report; if there be any virtue, and if there be any praise, think on these things"* (v.8 KJV).

That's enough to make us shout "Hallelujah!" But then Paul addresses two weighty issues (1) wealth and poverty; (2) giving and receiving.

The apostle tells the believers at Philippi, *"I have learned to be content, whatever the circumstances"* (v.11).

The word "content," as used in this context, means being independent of the outward circumstances based upon what is on the inside of your heart and soul. He learned to trust the Spirit of God within rather than the situation without.

My friend, we need to embrace this truth before we can truly understand seedtime and harvest. When this precept becomes part of your life, you will no longer be weary in well-doing.

Paul continues, *"I know both how to be abased* [humble], *and I know how to abound: every where and in all things I am instructed both to be full and to be hungry, both to abound and to suffer need"* (v.12 KJV).

Regardless of the situation, the apostle never lost sight of *Whose* he was.

------ ❧ ------

For Paul, whether he received material blessings or not wasn't the point. He knew God was his Source.

That is why he could declare, *"I can do everything through him who gives me strength"* (v.13).

Then, after commending the Christians for sharing in his travail, the apostle writes, *"Moreover, as you Philippians know, in the early days of your acquaintance with the gospel, when I set out from Macedonia, not one church shared with me in the matter of giving and receiving, except you only"* (v.15).

He talked of the time he was in dire need and they repeatedly sent him aid to Thessalonica. Then he adds these God-inspired words, *"Not that I am looking for a gift, but I am looking for what may be credited to your account"* (v.17).

Paul was saying, "I desired for souls to be saved and lives changed, and you gave—not because I didn't have food or clothing, but because you wanted me to be able to propagate the Gospel. And the only way I can do that is for my needs to be met."

Where was the credit applied? To the giver! (v.17).

Finally, Paul speaks of how their gifts multiplied and he was *"amply supplied"* with their *"fragrant offering, and acceptable sacrifice, pleasing to God"* (v.18).

Now the Lord would do the same for them as they did for Paul. He writes, *"My God will meet all your needs according to his glorious riches in Christ Jesus"* (v.19).

The positive things you pour into the lives of others, God will also grant unto you. Scripture declares that *"whatsoever good thing any man doeth, the same shall he receive of the Lord, whether he be bond or free"* (Ephesians 6:8 KJV).

You'll never find a better promise!

Release It!

I have heard people quote the verse "My God will meet all your needs" again and again without understanding its true meaning. You can repeat and affirm those words a thousand times, yet until you release seed into ministry for the Gospel's sake, the Lord will not respond.

*Let me encourage you to read
Paul's words until they penetrate
your very soul. They are a vital key
that unlocks God's blessing.*

The reason our church gives to missions and ministries is twofold: the Lord meets both their needs and ours. But if we hold onto what we have and do not release it (personally or as a church body) according to God's Word, we will remain where we are and stagnate.

Wealth of the Wicked

When I speak on this subject, someone invariably

asks, "Well, what about the person who doesn't live for God, yet seems to have incredible abundance?"

I point such a questioner to the first Psalm of David: *"Blessed is the man who does not walk in the counsel of the wicked or stand in the way of sinners or sit in the seat of mockers. But his delight is in the law of the Lord, and on his law he meditates day and night. He is like a tree planted by streams of water, which yields its fruit in season and whose leaf does not wither. Whatever he does prospers. Not so the wicked! They are like chaff that the wind blows away. Therefore the wicked will not stand in the judgment, nor sinners in the assembly of the righteous. For the Lord watches over the way of the righteous, but the way of the wicked will perish"* (Psalms 1:1-6).

I can't deplete my energy and time being unduly concerned what the ungodly are doing because they are driving down a dead end road. Everyone has a season and God says, "Don't worry about the ungodly. They're doomed! Their season is short lived."

When you sow into good soil (God's soil), your time of harvest will come and it will be everlasting—perpetual.

The Day of Reckoning

Somehow I found myself on the mailing list of a radio minister who railed against "faith" preachers and those who believe God wants His children to prosper —he even published a booklet on the topic. Yet he sent me a letter saying, "We need for you to prayerfully consider sending us twenty dollars or we are going to go off the air."

Why would I sow into the ministry of one who doesn't believe in the seed of harvest? Even more incredible, this radio preacher lived a luxurious lifestyle and flew in a personal jet plane. He obviously didn't want others to prosper—just himself. But a day of reckoning will come.

Unfortunately, a mentality has crept into the church which tells us we are to give not expecting God to do anything in return, but our Heavenly Father has a much different viewpoint. He says, "If you are willing to give, I must replenish you since there are so few people like you who will support My work."

Remember, *"He who gives to the poor will lack nothing"* (Proverbs 28:27).

Act on Your Faith

I believe the Lord desires to bless the *entire* Body

of Christ. If I read the book of Acts correctly, it records that the early believers began to sell their possessions and give to those who had a need—so the church would be fortified and strong (Acts 2:44-45).

Do you realize what this means? As a result of their sacrifice, everyone in the church had a roof over their head, clothes on their back and food on their table while together they spread the Good News.

It was a graphic demonstration of seedtime and harvest, mirroring the words of the psalmist, *"I have been young, and now am old; yet have I not seen the righteous forsaken, nor his seed begging bread"* (Psalms 37:25 KJV).

Here is the result of those who shared fellowship together and praised God. They enjoyed the favor of the people and *"the Lord added to their number daily those who were being saved"* (Acts 2:47).

When you release your substance, you make a declaration God sees and hears. It is then He pours out a harvest beyond measure.

Little or Much?

Not only is it important *what* you plant, but *how*.

I like the words of John Bunyan, the author of Pilgrim's Progress. He wrote, "There was a man, some called him mad; the more he gave, the more he had."

That is biblical!

Let me call your attention to an important passage: *"Remember this: Whoever sows sparingly will also reap sparingly, and whoever sows generously will also reap generously. Each man should give what he has decided in his heart to give, not reluctantly or under compulsion, for God loves a cheerful giver. And God is able to make all grace abound to you, so that in all things at all times, having all that you need, you will abound in every good work. As it is written: 'He has scattered abroad his gifts to the poor; his righteousness endures forever.' Now he who supplies seed to the sower and bread for food will also supply and increase your store of seed and will enlarge the harvest of your righteousness"* (2 Corinthians 9:6-10).

Most people focus on the words, "Each man should give what he has decided in his heart to give." They would rather not dwell on the fact the Lord says, "Whoever sows sparingly will also reap sparingly."

God's principles can't be ignored, yet they are by so many well-intentioned believers.

Oh, we can quote scripture and verse that declares, *"if thou shalt confess with thy mouth the Lord Jesus, and shalt believe in thine heart that God hath raised him from the dead, thou shalt be saved"* (Romans 10:9 KJV.) And, *"as many as received him* [Jesus], *to them gave he power to become the sons of God, even to them that believe on his name"* (John 1:12 KJV).

Yet, if we teach that when you give according to God's plan you should expect to receive His blessing, we are branded as heretics.

Didn't the Lord give His Son with the belief that people would receive Jesus and come back into God's family? He *gave* in order to receive—and the Bible says we are to act like Him. *"Be imitators of God, therefore, as dearly loved children"* (Ephesians 5:1).

If we are going to <u>be</u> like the Lord, we must <u>act</u> like Him.

God so loved the world He gave, expecting to receive a harvest!

What Will You Reap?

The law of seedtime and harvest is universal; it applies to both saint and sinner alike.

Here is how the apostle Paul explains it: *"Do not be deceived: God cannot be mocked. A man reaps what he sows.*

The one who sows to please his sinful nature, from that nature will reap destruction; the one who sows to please the Spirit, from the Spirit will reap eternal life" (Galatians 6:7-8).

If you think this message only concerns money, you've come to the wrong conclusion. This scripture tells us if we sow strictly for personal gain and fleshly lust, we will reap corruption. It's a matter of attitude.

Stop making excuses for not walking in the fullness of a loving, generous God. Start sowing in the Spirit, and be ready to reap life everlasting.

CHAPTER 3

THE MIRACLE OF A SEED

As you open your Bible and delve into scripture, like an archeologist, you can uncover hidden treasures. It's happened to me time after time.

One of the great gems I have found is that when you interpret a truth of God's Word it applies to your spirit, soul and body. Not just one or two dimensions, but all three! If it is not applicable in all realms, it is not truth and you have misinterpreted the scripture.

What transpires in the spirit arena is what controls the natural arena—and if it's true in the spirit, it has to be true in the flesh.

I've heard believers say, "Well, I'm healed in spirit, but not in body. That will take place in the sweet by and by!"

According to God's Word, I don't know how you can come to such a conclusion. It's a man-made dogma.

Here is another question I am frequently asked. "Pastor, I know so many good people who are sick and hurting. They don't seem to be walking in victory the way they should. Why?"

It's a natural question—with a supernatural answer.

If you already possess abundance in the form of the seed, then your supply for tomorrow can start with whatever you hold in your hand today. It's a miraculous process!

You're Already There!

Why is it people fail to walk in healing, prosperity, peace of mind, or in the blessing Christ has already provided? We must come to the place where we know that tomorrow's harvest begins with what is in our possession today. And that seed must be planted in receptive soil.

I can't wait until next month or next year to believe God for something specific. I must have faith and expectation, and act on it this day!

Most individuals are guilty of waiting until they are neck-deep in problems before calling on God—only then do they exercise their belief. If that's the case, they are not demonstrating absolute trust in the things of God. They are just screaming out for mercy, living in fear rather than faith.

Remember, fear doesn't move God—only faith does!

A man who hadn't worked for three weeks suddenly panicked, realizing that in seven days his house payment was due. So, at the start of the fourth week he began searching for work, moaning and complaining, "Why God, why? Please, You've got to help me. Help me now."

This man should have been exercising his faith the first week, not the last!

Now is the Time!

Don't wait until you face a crisis before believing God and acting on His Word.

**What you already possess
has the potential to produce
an incredible harvest.**

Release it now—by making a phone call, knocking on a door, perhaps even giving a gift! What occurs in the flesh germinates the seed in the soul and spirit. They're inexplicably connected. Yet, if you hesitate or delay, you place your tomorrows in jeopardy.

If you travel through life with the attitude, "I'm

going to wait for someone to be friendly to me first before I reciprocate," you'll spend many lonely years wondering why no one befriends you. That's the world's approach.

Start being a "today" person.

Begin by saying, "My supply for tomorrow is found and released in what I do with my seed right now."

These are not idle words. They are based on God's eternal principle.

What Do You See?

Your solution may be closer than you think. With childlike belief, wrap your faith around your seed and your seed around your need.

God's law of seedtime and harvest is a physical truth established within a spiritual principle.

As we find from Genesis to Revelation, nothing is manifested in the natural which has not already been ordained in the spiritual. If it is not inherent in what we have *not* seen, it won't be evident in that which we physically see.

At a place called Dothan, the prophet Elisha was

surrounded by a large army, ready to strike. His servant was trembling with fear, saying, *"Oh, my lord, what shall we do?"* (2 Kings 6:15).

Elisha answered, *"Don't be afraid...those who are with us are more than those who are with them."* (v.16). Then the prophet prayed, *"O Lord, open his eyes so he may see"* (v.17).

When the servant's eyes were opened by God, he saw the hills full of horses, chariots and armies of the Lord—and *"fire all around Elisha"* (v.17).

What caused the dramatic difference? His spiritual eyes were made clear! For the first time He was able to visibly see God's fighting forces—the angels and the army of the Lord!

This scene didn't suddenly manifest itself because the servants eyes were opened. God's army had been there all the time!

In the New Testament, the apostle Paul tells us, *"...we fix our eyes not on what is seen, but on what is unseen. For what is seen is temporary, but what is unseen is eternal"* (2 Corinthians 4:18).

What About Our Needs?

Seedtime and harvest is a *physical* thing, but since it has been ordained by God Himself, it is a spiritual principle—something the Creator established.

We also must realize that *needs* do not create a

harvest. Some people sow only when they are trapped in a desperate situation, but necessity is not the qualifier. If that were true, India would probably be the most blessed nation on earth. Or we could look at the famines of Africa and expect a harvest in Ethiopia or the Sudan.

> *Please understand, it is not a sin to have a need, but according to the Word, it is an abomination if you do nothing about it.*

The Bible declares, *"Therefore to him that knoweth to do good, and doeth it not, to him it is sin"* (James 4:17 KJV).

Perhaps *you* will become the seed that brings life to people who have lost all hope. God's Word promises *"if you spend yourselves in behalf of the hungry and satisfy the needs of the oppressed, then your light will rise in the darkness, and your night will become like the noonday. The Lord will guide you always; he will satisfy your needs in a sun-scorched land and will strengthen your frame. You will be like a well-watered garden, like a spring whose waters never fail"* (Isaiah 58:10-11).

Remember, only God can turn night into day.

Who is Responsible?

Everything I am today and everything I will be tomorrow is based upon the seeds that I sow and those I receive. What I give out and what I allow to be sown in me, establishes my life.

- I can't blame society.
- I can't blame the government or the economy.
- I can't blame my father, mother or my brother.
- I can't blame the body of Christ.

I can still bring to mind a teen in our youth group who was extremely gifted at getting into trouble. But to him, nothing was ever his fault. He didn't have a kind word to say about anyone. After gently trying to change his behavior, I finally called him in and said, "Listen, young man, if you don't change your negative ways, you are headed for disaster!"

"What do you mean?" he brusquely wanted to know.

I responded, "Without asking the Lord to change your spirit, there is no way you can fit into this group because everything you do is blamed on others. You have not taken responsibility for yourself."

I prayed the Lord would get his attention.

You see, this young man was planting seeds of turmoil in those around him, and I feared for the devastating crop it could produce.

Three Seeds

There is so much more involved with sowing and reaping than sitting in a pew and placing a check in the offering plate. Let me give you three examples:

1. Prayer is a seed.

When we talk to the Lord one-on-one from the depths of our innermost being, we are sowing into His Kingdom.

We pray for two reasons: (1) to worship and have fellowship with the Father and (2) to ask the Lord to meet our needs. Thank God, it's not a one way conversation. He talks back to us and answers our prayers—and the process is based on seedtime and harvest.

God declares, *"He will call upon me, and I will answer him"* (Psalms 91:15).

Jesus, in His Sermon on the Mount, says, *"But when you pray, go into your room, close the door and pray to your Father, who is unseen. Then your Father, who sees what is done in secret, will reward you."* (Matthew 6:6).

2. Studying God's Word is a seed.

It is impossible to invest your time in meditating

on the Word without realizing a harvest in your life.

Every deposit we make produces results— whether for good or bad. That's why David says, *"I have hidden your word in my heart that I might not sin against you"* (Psalms 119:11).

If you are struggling with temptation and sin, don't search for some spiritual giant to take authority over that spirit. The answer is as close as the Holy Bible.

Begin to soak your life thoroughly with scripture —word by word, verse by verse, chapter by chapter. You are depositing seed that will spring up as a glorious harvest.

God gives you this command followed by a promise, *"Do not let this Book of the Law depart from your mouth; meditate on it day and night, so that you may be careful to do everything written in it. Then you will be prosperous and successful"* (Joshua 1:8).

3. Sharing your faith is a seed.

Every time you share with someone the love of Jesus, you are making a spiritual deposit into their life—and yours!

We are all workers in God's field and He expects us

to be faithful. For example, the apostle Paul did the work of an evangelist, but there were leaders in the local church, such as Apollos, who edified the converts Paul had won. That's why he writes, *"...the Lord has assigned to each his task. I planted the seed, Apollos watered it, but God made it grow"* (1 Corinthians 3:6). And Paul adds, *"The man who plants and the man who waters have one purpose, and each will be rewarded according to his own labor"* (1 Corinthians 3:8).

Don't Quit Now!

A woman recently told me, "I've been witnessing to my neighbor for six months and there appears to be absolutely zero response. I am getting so weary. It seems as though I am talking to myself and I am ready to quit!"

Perhaps you have found yourself in a similar situation.

It's time for a new perspective. Your words are not falling on deaf ears—you are in the center of God's will, sowing seeds.

What does Paul tell us? *"Let us not become weary in doing good, for at the proper time we will reap a harvest if we do not give up"* (Galatians 6:9).

Just as a baby isn't born at the moment of conception, it takes time for what is planted to germinate. But "due season" is coming!

Never become frustrated and exhausted giving of your time, talent, finances or your energy, even if you feel your efforts are falling on fallow ground. According to the Word, what you have planted will live. Jesus says, *"I tell you the truth, unless a kernel of wheat falls to the ground and dies, it remains only a single seed. But if it dies, it produces many seeds"* (John 12:24).

Sharing Christ is part of the great ingathering He spoke about so often. Jesus said to the disciples, *"The harvest is plentiful but the workers are few. Ask the Lord of the harvest, therefore, to send out workers into his harvest field"* (Matthew 9:37-38).

This means me! This means you!

CHAPTER 4

10 PRINCIPLES OF SOWING

Many of the great problems facing our world are the result of failed stewardship. We have not taken seriously what God has given us or used it properly.

At creation, when God formed man and woman, He blessed them and said, *"Be fruitful, and multiply, and replenish the earth, and subdue it: and have dominion over the fish of the sea, and over the fowl of the air, and over every living thing that moveth upon the earth"* (Genesis 1:28 KJV).

What has been the result of this *dominion?* Millions have been living and suffering with wars, famine and poverty.

As individuals, we have abused our responsibility by sowing to the flesh rather than to the spirit—and we wonder why everything is in such disarray.

It is amazing to me that people want everything

God has to offer to them, yet they don't want to live by His covenants. They'd rather hum the Frank Sinatra song, "I did it my way!"

From my pulpit, I have asked:

- "How many want God's hand on their lives?"
  Every believer responds, "Yeah, Lord!"
- "How many want the spirit of God to be present in a mighty way?"
  "Amen!"
- "How many want signs and wonders to flow through them?"
  "Yes, yes!"
- "How many want the blessings of God demonstrated physically and tangibly?"
  "Yeah, Lord!"
- "How many are willing to live holy and righteous before God?"
  "We'll think about it, Lord."

They hesitate and are reluctant to act upon the very thing that is the key to their harvest. The Bible declares, *"For the Lord God is a sun and shield: the Lord will give grace and glory: no good thing will he withhold from them that walk uprightly"* (Psalms 84:11).

We all want to feast at the banquet table, yet God continues to ask, "What have you done with what I have given? How are you planting your seed?"

Let me share these ten principles of sowing:

1. Seedtime and harvest must become a lifestyle.

This is not something you occasionally practice in an attempt to have the Lord bless a business venture or a member of your family. It must be a 24/7 total lifestyle encompassing everything you do.

In the natural, each move we make produces some kind of response. According to Newton's Third Law of Motion—for every action there is an equal and opposite reaction.

God's law of the harvest will be in force for as long as time remains.

For this reason we must move into the rhythm and pattern of sowing good seed, nurturing the plant and reaping the results. It should become an automatic outcome of our stewardship and lifestyle.

2. Every word you speak is a seed sown.

What flows out of the mouth not only reveals the content of your heart, it determines the course of your life.

Our words can help or hinder, bless or curse, heal or hurt, and, according to the Word, *"The tongue has the power of life and death"* (Proverbs 18:21).

I trust you understand that what you are doing today is a direct result of the words you spoke yesterday, last month or years ago. This is what the Lord set into motion from the beginning – He *spoke*, and the world was created.

God not only gave us dominion over the world, but over our tongue!

Today, when we speak with righteousness, faith and under the inspiration of the Holy Spirit, we are sowing the kind of seed God blesses.

3. You must constantly look for the harvest.

I have met people who say they expect to reap, yet they certainly don't demonstrate it. When something unfortunate takes place, they respond, "I knew that was going to happen!"

Obviously, they were looking for the wrong harvest!

Friend, anything negative should be considered abnormal.

I learned in elementary school that if I hit a

classmate, he was probably going to hit me back. Again, it's the law of action and reaction. So I had to determine what kind of seed I would use to give me leverage over those bigger kids.

We must "see" the results we desire—and count the cost of receiving them.

Start looking! *"Say not ye, There are yet four months, and then cometh harvest? behold, I say unto you, Lift up your eyes, and look on the fields; for they are white already to harvest"* (John 4:35 KJV).

4. Recognize that the law of the harvest is God's truth, not yours.

Some like to write the rules for receiving the Lord's blessing. They want to select the type of seed, the condition of the soil, even the planting and watering schedule. Then, when they fail to receive the expected results, they grumble and complain.

It's time to recognize the fact we are living on God's land, not ours. He owns both the field and the yield!

The best way to plant is to begin by falling to your knees—literally. Prayerfully ask God's direction before you separate the soil and tap in the tiny seed. The only "Farmer's Almanac" you'll ever need is the Bible. It reveals the *what, when, where* and *how* of sowing.

5. Begin planting your seed where you are.

We have all heard the excuses:

- "One of these days I'm going to begin saving for my future."
- "I know I should be teaching a Sunday School class, but I'm too busy this year."
- "I have a cousin I sure wish someone would witness to."

Do we really want a harvest? If so, we must start here—and *now!* We cannot wait until everything is right and conditions are perfect.

If you are believing God to bless you financially yet you don't have money to sow, start with something that is of value to you.

If you are praying for the Lord to touch a friend's life, decide you will be the instrument He uses.

If you believe God answers prayer, start praying. Begin where you are. *"I tell you, now is the time of God's favor"* (2 Corinthians 6:2).

6. Realize that you are promised a harvest.

Here's a question I want you to think about: What would you do if you knew you could not fail?

Would you launch a new business or decide to become a singer? Go into the ministry?

When I was asked that same question, I answered, "I would be faithful to whatever I put my hand to, knowing it would prosper."

This is more than an assumption. When you walk in God's will and plant the seed of His choosing, you cannot fail. He promises a time of reaping for *"As long as the earth endures"* (Genesis 8:22).

If you are faithful to sow the seed, the Lord is faithful to give you a harvest.

7. Should your crop fail, ask God to help you begin again.

As believers, we all make mistakes, but that doesn't mean we should stop reading the Bible and abandon the church.

The Lord allows us to start again.

Remember Jonah? God told him to plant the Word in the city of Nineveh, yet he rebelled and departed for Tarsus. After being thrown overboard and swallowed by the whale, this servant of God came to his senses. That's when the fish had indigestion and threw him up on dry ground. *"Then the word of the Lord came to Jonah a second time: 'Go to the great city of Nineveh and proclaim to it the message I give you'"* (Jonah 3:1-2).

God gave him a second chance.

The same was true of Peter—who became a tragic failure by publicly denying the Lord. Yet, after the resurrection, Peter was the first person Jesus came looking for. He was forgiven and began planting the Gospel into the lives of thousands.

8. Recognize that seedtime and harvest is meant for your good.

God's promise is not for someone else; it is for you. Just because your season of abundance has not arrived doesn't mean it will never come.

It is a *good* thing to believe the Lord will bring you a harvest because it is a "God principle" that has been set in motion. You have to believe *in* it and *for* it!

Your Father says, *"Give, and it will be given to you"* (Luke 6:38). That's a divine promise.

9. Believe God will increase what you have given.

When you clutch a tiny seed in your hand, it could easily slip through your fingers, but try planting and watering it in fertile soil and watch what happens. It develops a life of its own. That one seed begins to multiply—giving you food to eat and enough left over to sow an even larger crop.

God's Word declares, *"Now he who supplies seed to the sower and bread for food will also supply and increase your store of seed and will enlarge the harvest of your righteousness"* (2 Corinthians 9:10).

The Lord doesn't add, He multiplies!

10. Understand that seedtime and harvest is based on specific seasons.

After the flood, God instituted winter, spring, summer and fall, and this pattern has never changed. There is an appointed time to sow and a time to reap.

No farmer would plant a seed in the ground one day and come back the next demanding, "Where is my crop?" No, he waits until the season of harvest.

As a young boy, Joseph had a dream that he would one day be a leader. Even after being sold into slavery and sent to Egypt, he patiently waited until the moment arrived when his vision became a reality. It happened in God's time, not Joseph's!

The Coming Harvest

What kind of stewards have we been with the seed God has placed in our hand? Has it been scattered or sown, wasted or watered, ravaged or reaped?

One day soon we will all give an account for the actions of our life. At the final harvest, I want to hear my Father say, "Well done!"

CHAPTER 5

START DIGGING!

In my book, *Capturing the Mind of God*, I mentioned an unexpected meeting I had with Dr. Oral Roberts in 1991. Let me tell you why that encounter was important and how it impacts what you are now reading.

I was about to return from Tulsa, Oklahoma, while serving on the Board of Regents at Oral Roberts University. The phone rang in my hotel room with a call from his secretary, saying, "Dr. Roberts is flying down to South Florida. Would you like to travel back with him on the corporate jet?"

I didn't say, "Let me pray about it!" Of course not, I responded with an enthusiastic, "Yes!"

On board were Oral and Evelyn Roberts along with Jim and Lucy Blanchett, also Regents at ORU.

I had never really been around Dr. Roberts on such an informal one-on-one level. Oh, I'd been in meetings with him and he had even spoken at our church, yet this was my first chance for a relaxed, personal conversation.

What Would I Ask?

To be honest, I was quite nervous. After all, I was a new member of the Board of Regents and didn't want to embarrass myself. In those first meetings I decided to be as quiet as possible—listening and learning.

Now on board the jet, I was thinking to myself, "What am I going to talk about with Dr. Roberts?"

I don't know about you, but when I am around certain people, I don't want to waste time because you never know when you will have such an opportunity again.

———✣———

I wondered, "What can I ask him that will not make me sound foolish, and at the same time give him an opportunity to talk?"

In reality, all I wanted was to hear what he had to say, and I didn't really care about the subject matter. After all, he was a spiritual giant to me.

Calculating what I was going to say, I finally

thought of one good question. "I'll ask him what he can tell me, as a young pastor, that would help me understand where the Body of Christ has missed the mark." I thought, "This is going to be good for at least 30 or 40 minutes!"

The Challenge

Dr. Roberts, casually dressed in a jogging suit and sneakers, slowly unwrapped a piece of candy when I posed the question. In anticipation, I thought, "Okay, I am about to receive some great wisdom concerning where the church has strayed off course."

Finally, he took his candy out of the wrapper, and after struggling with it for a few seconds, looked over at me and said, "They leave their harvest in the field."

Then he popped the candy in his mouth and started enjoying it.

This took me by surprise and I asked, "Well, what do you mean by that?"—watching as he opened a second piece of candy.

"Look it up for yourself," he nonchalantly replied.

Then he shut his eyes and did not utter another word to me until we landed at Fort Lauderdale.

I thought to myself, "Why such a short answer? Was he tired? Is he annoyed with me?" No. Instantly, I knew he was giving me a challenge.

The minute I returned home, I began fervently

seeking God and searching the scripture on the subject of seedtime and harvest.

Out of that brief encounter with Oral Roberts and a deepening relationship with the Lord, God opened my heart to a message that has been central to my ministry.

On the Same Page

Since that time, I've had the privilege of talking with Dr. Roberts on numerous occasions. When we recalled the short conversation on the plane, he laughed and said, "Now you understand!" And I did.

Over the years I have been able to glean some incredible riches from the Bible on this topic. You see, I was challenged to dig into the Word so that Dr. Roberts and I would be on the same page.

Basically, what he was saying to me earlier was, "You won't find what you're looking for unless you dig it out of the Word for yourself!"

Your Seed of Faith

There are millions of church members content to let others provide answers, yet they have never done their homework. As a result, God's Word has not been effectively sown in their hearts. They have never absorbed His truth.

Some question why today there is such a lack of

provision and miracles operating in the Body of Christ. I believe it is because Christians *say* what they believe, yet they don't really *know* it. They have not hidden God's Word in their hearts.

Is it any wonder that in times of turmoil people lack an anchor for their soul? God's mercy is marvelous, yet the Bible tells us, *"The just shall live by faith"* (Romans 1:17 KJV).

What is the source of such faith? Does it come simply from attending church or talking with a minister. No. The scripture declares that *"faith cometh by hearing, and hearing by the word of God"* (Romans 10:17 KJV).

Storming Heaven's Gates!

Perseverance and diligence are required ingredients for both our study of the Word and our prayer life.

If someone handed you a dollar for every hour you have spent on your knees before the Lord, would you be rich or poor?

Weight lifters and body builders train with the slogan, "No pain, no gain." In other words, if you're not willing to pay the price by sweating in the gym, you'll never enjoy the benefits.

As believers, if we are not prepared to storm the gates of heaven, why should we expect God to pour out His blessings and answer when we call?

Fervent! Intense!

Have you experienced the dynamic difference between simply reciting words or coming before the Lord with a heartfelt prayer—a cry that has incredible meaning to you?

I'm not talking about, "Now I lay me down to sleep," or "God bless Mom and Dad." Rather, it is a communion with God, filled with such passion and commitment, you will not rise from your knees until you have entered into His glorious presence.

The Bible says, *"The effectual fervent prayer of a righteous man availeth much"* (James 5:16 KJV).

On a scale of one to ten, how would you rate the intensity of your prayer life?

Friend, if you could create a harvest through your own abilities, you wouldn't need God. For this reason, He places us in a position that requires us to search for Him. He *"is a rewarder of them that diligently seek him"* (Hebrews 11:6 KJV).

Six Hours a Day?

Another privilege of my life was to talk with Dr. Paul Yongi Cho, pastor of one of the world's largest churches in Seoul, Korea. This saint of God spends a minimum of four hours every day of his life in prayer.

However, he told me, "When I come to the States, sometimes I have to pray six hours each day, because your demonic activities are much greater than in Korea."

It comes as no surprise to me that God has blessed this prayer warrior abundantly. He has built a congregation of several hundred thousand people.

Prayer opens the door for the Lord to begin working not just for us, but through us. As Paul writes, *"Now to him who is able to do immeasurably more than all we ask or imagine, according to his power that is at work within us"* (Ephesians 3:20).

The Coming Exam

There's no alternative for focus and concentration.

A college student who is not willing to put in the required hours of listening to lectures, taking notes, reading the assignments and digesting the material will be embarrassed when it's time for final exams. Why? Because you can't take out what you have not put in!

Don't expect to reap an "A" when you have planted an "F."

Paying the Price

You may say, "But Pastor, I'm sure you understand that we are not saved by works of righteousness, rather by God's mercy and grace. It's free. There's no price to be paid!"

Wait just a moment. Someone *did* pay a great price.

While it's true we are redeemed by grace, it cost the Father everything! It was paid for in an awesome way.

I cannot over-emphasize that God so loved the world that He *gave* His only begotten Son. Jesus was a seed that guaranteed the salvation of humanity—and it was purchased by His precious blood on Calvary. *"You were bought at a price"* (1 Corinthians 7:23).

Planting the Word

Everything in life requires a seed. If your marriage

is going to be successful, then you must invest in the relationship. It's not what you extract; it's what you deposit!

The same principle applies when reaching people for Christ. Someone must first plant the Word before a soul is redeemed. Paul writes, *"How, then, can they call on the one they have not believed in? And how can they believe in the one of whom they have not heard? And how can they hear without someone preaching to them?"* (Romans 10:14).

The Right Tools

The Lord has given us the seeds to be extraordinary achievers. In fact, He believes we are not simply conquerors, but *"more than conquerors"* (Romans 8:37 KJV).

God says, "I have given you the tools to accomplish far more than you can ever achieve in the natural."

Start digging!

CHAPTER 6

GIVE IT AWAY!

No doubt you have crossed the path of those who live by the carefree words of the song made famous by Doris Day, "Que sera, sera. Whatever will be, will be."

In reality, however, that is not the case. What you become is not determined by happenstance or fate, rather by your actions of yesterday and today—seeds you have sown during your lifetime.

Pass it On!

Years ago I heard a minister comment, "God will give it *to* you if He can get it *through* you."

We are all trustees of this planet—temporary custodians of the Lord's earthly kingdom while we are passing through. What a privilege He has granted us.

Everything God has loaned to us is for a reason. It is not so we can flaunt our possessions or positions, bragging, "Look at me!" No. It's been given to us so we can be a blessing to someone else.

That's what the Lord told Abraham: *"I will bless*

you..and all peoples on earth will be blessed through you" (Genesis 12:2-3).

If you are sincere about developing the lifestyle of a sower, the Lord will make certain you have something to sow—and will provide even if it takes a miracle.

"Don't Eat Your Seed!"

Not only will God furnish "starter" seed, He will sustain you. The Lord gives *"bread for food"* (2 Corinthians 9:10).

There's a phrase I heard years ago that has always stuck with me: *Don't eat your seed!*

Some people look at what is in their hand and say, "Hallelujah, I'm going down to the car dealer and buy a new BMW!"

Seed is for planting, not squandering. But you say, "How am I going to survive until my crops are ready to harvest? Stop worrying! If you are obeying God, He will supply you with exactly what you need during the growing season.

Listen closely, and you will hear Him encouraging you to have patience—*"...never tire of doing what is right"* (2 Thessalonians 3:13). The season of reaping is on its way!

The Bible says, *"Do not muzzle an ox while it is treading out the grain"* (Deuteronomy 25:4). In other words, God wants you to keep working, participating in the process until the harvest arrives—as long as you're willing to take the seed of that harvest and sow it again.

Be Willing to Change

I want to remind you Satan is constantly on the prowl, doing everything in his power to belittle you. He wants you to believe there is absolutely nothing you can contribute to the lives of others. Don't listen to his lies!

The Bible declares if you are a sower, God will supply the seed—He will deliver it to you regardless of the barriers. Never forget that He *"supplies seed to the sower"* (2 Corinthians 9:10).

If you are unhappy with the crop you are reaping, don't despair—ask yourself, "What do I need to do differently?" Start planting in a fresh field!

God will perform something new in your life if you are willing to stretch your faith and venture into areas you have never been before.

———✦———

Why should we expect the Lord to move if we aren't willing to change?

Your Father's Watching

God is recording every step you take – how you speak and the way you act and react. He bases what He does for you on *you!*

You may ask, "Isn't God sovereign...unchangeable?"

Of course, He is – especially concerning His Word. He declares, *"I will hasten my word to perform it"* (Jeremiah 1:12 KJV).

However, throughout scripture the Almighty deals with each individual according to their behavior. For example, God chose David to be king of Israel because He found in him, *"a man after mine own heart, which shall fulfil all my will"* (Acts 13:22 KJV). Yet, when David committed a horrible sin with Bathsheba, God said, *"I am going to bring calamity on you, "* (2 Samuel 12:11). If you keep reading you will find that David repented and the Lord forgave, showering him once again with blessings.

Like every good father, God uses opportunities of discipline and rewards to shape our eternal destiny.

Who Comes First?

Your Heavenly Father is not worried concerning your material possessions unless they obstruct or hinder the path of blessings He intends to flow through you.

Someone arrives at church in a brand new car equipped with all the bells and whistles and the tongues begin to wag. "Well, you know, he doesn't really *need* that vehicle."

Making decisions based on need means different things to different people. For example, I could say, "Why do you need a new shirt when the ones you bought last year look just fine!" Or, "Why did you eat at that upscale steak house? Wouldn't a Burger King do?"

I believe the Lord has no problem with you enjoying the fruit of your labor as long as you place Him first.

A Rolls Royce?

A few years ago I played golf with Bill Swad, a Christian businessman from Columbus, Ohio, who has greatly prospered with his car dealerships.

He arrived to pick me up in a yellow Rolls Royce. A few minutes down the road we were having a light-hearted conversation when I turned to him and asked, "Bill, has anybody ever given you a hard time about driving a Rolls Royce?"

He thought for a moment and replied, "Yes, I had one man come up to me who was rather angry and said, 'How can you drive such an ostentatious car. Why don't you sell it and give the money to God's Kingdom?'"

Bill told the man, "Are you willing to get your checkbook out if I do the same—and compare our giving? If you have given an equivalent of what I have over the years—based upon the percentage of our incomes—then I'll sell the Rolls Royce."

The gentleman was forming his opinion on what he saw, not on the facts. He was unaware Swad has contributed millions of dollars to Christian ministries in this nation and around the world. He wasn't squandering, but enjoying a small fraction of his earthly harvest.

_____ ～❧ _____

The Lord's priority is this: "What have you done with what I have placed in your hand?"

It's the people who *don't have* who complain. The spirit of envy and jealousy spurs them to say, "If I can't have it, you shouldn't either!"

An Expensive Hobby

Every person views the world through their own perspective and makes decisions based on their personal priorities.

I certainly don't drive a Rolls, but once when I purchased a new car, an acquaintance casually commented, "Preacher, I just couldn't live with myself if I spent money on a car like that."

The man invited us over to his home and I noticed he had a collection of guns on display. "Tell me about these," I asked, curiously.

With great pleasure, he began to share the history and details of each of his prized firearms—even saying how much they cost.

As I sat there, I began to chuckle to myself. His hobby cost more than my car! I thought about the scripture, *"Do not answer a fool according to his folly, or you will be like him yourself"* (Proverbs 26:4).

While what we value may differ, God deals with each of his children based on our hearts.

Your Unique Purpose

When Mother Teresa was alive, every dollar that passed through her hands she put into her hospital for the needy of Calcutta. It was her passion to reach the suffering children of India.

Yet, what would happen if every believer said, "That's what I am going to do; sell everything I own and spend my life as a foreign missionary.

While that sounds noble, think of the consequences:

- We would never have the funds to build another church.
- We would never be salt and light to those in the corporate world.
- Our witness to children and teens in this nation would end.

Just as a peach pit doesn't produce pears, the Lord places something unique within you for a specific purpose. Some are raised to be athletes, others go into teaching, administration, government, high finance or medicine.

For each of these callings, God says, "I'll supply seed to fulfill the purpose for which I have called you."

Stop worrying about what others are doing—that is between them and God.

Hedged In!

My uncle Hugh was an alcoholic and my parents not only prayed for him, they *gave* to him. But before helping, they always prayed with each other, "In the name of Jesus, we're sowing the seed that's going to bring about his salvation."

You certainly can't buy redemption, but these prayers paid big dividends. Along the way, Uncle Hugh was hedged in. Everywhere he turned someone was telling him about Jesus.

When he laid his head on his pillow at night, he said, "I could hear the Lord speaking to me."

My uncle couldn't escape because there was a family constantly sowing prayer, support and encouragement into his life—and witnessing to him about the Savior.

Before he left this earth, Uncle Hugh had a marvelous conversion, giving his life to Christ and leading others to the Lord.

There are instances where it takes more to win the lost than simply saying, "Jesus loves you." We need to give of ourselves—visibly showing our care and concern rather than lambasting people with hellfire and brimstone.

People of Blessing

Earlier we talked of Abraham—how God said that

both he and his seed would be a blessing to the nations. Those words are meant for us! *"If you belong to Christ, then you are Abraham's seed, and heirs according to the promise"* (Galatians 3:29).

> ### *We must see ourselves as <u>people of blessing</u>; which means everywhere we go we are touching lives on behalf of the Lord – bringing His blessings with us.*

What a difference from the unsaved individual who says, "How much can I get out of this person? What can they do for me?"

Start asking, "How many people can I *bless* with God's love today?"

Exercise Your Faith

If you have joined a local church and are faithful with your attendance and support, I commend you. But I feel compelled to ask, " What are you doing with the incredible Word of God that is being planted into your life from the pulpit?"

_____ 🌿 _____

*In order to grow in grace, we
must exercise our faith. This means
we receive the Word, comprehend and
study it, then turn around and
share it with someone else.*

Again, God says, "I will give seed to the *sower*." It's not yours to keep. Today, don't worry concerning how much seed you possess, ask, "How much have I given away?"

CHAPTER 7

DON'T DIVIDE, MULTIPLY!

I f you want to learn the secret of heaven's blessings, start at the beginning of the Book. The first words out of God's mouth when He created Adam and Eve were, *"Be fruitful and multiply"* (Genesis 1:22 KJV).

After the great flood the Lord blessed Noah and his sons, then He repeated those same words, *"Be fruitful, and multiply, and replenish the earth"* (Genesis 9:1 KJV).

This principle applies to everything God created—man, animal life and vegetation. For example, a seed doesn't just produce another seed—it *multiplies.*

More Than Enough!

Have you ever "unshucked" an ear of corn? There's not just one kernel on the cob, but hundreds—even up to a thousand!

What's even more amazing is, each one of those kernels are actually seeds that can be planted to produce a stalk with several more ears of corn and thousands more seeds.

It's the miracle of plant life:

- One apple seed can grow a tree that will produce enough to make over 225 apple pies a year—perpetually.
- The face of the average sunflower contains 3,000 seeds.
- From one seed grows a watermelon which produces approximately 1,000 seeds. If each were planted, you'd have 1 million watermelons—in just the second generation.

Mustard Seed Faith!

The Gospel of Matthew records an incident when Jesus was ministering with His disciples. In one large crowd, a man approached Jesus and knelt before Him, pleading, *"Lord, have mercy on my son...He has seizures and is suffering greatly. He often falls into the fire or into the water. I brought him to your disciples, but they could not heal him"* (Matthew 17:15-16).

Chastising the entire throng which had gathered around Him, Jesus replied, *"O unbelieving and perverse generation ...how long shall I stay with you? How long shall I put up with you? Bring the boy here to me"* (Matthew v.17).

Jesus rebuked the demon; it came out of the boy, and he was delivered—set completely free that very moment.

Then the disciples asked Jesus in private, *"Why couldn't we drive it out?"* (v.19).)

He answered, *"Because you have so little faith. I tell you the truth, if you have faith as small as a mustard seed, you can say to this mountain, 'Move from here to there' and it will move. Nothing will be impossible for you"* (v.20).

What a revelation! God can use any amount of faith, regardless of size.

Do you know how minute a mustard seed really is? Yet, just a small handful is enough to grow hundreds of trees.

Jesus used a similar example when He said, *"The kingdom of heaven is like a mustard seed, which a man took and planted in his field. Though it is the smallest of all your seeds, yet when it grows, it is the largest of garden plants and becomes a tree, so that the birds of the air come and perch in its branches"* (Matthew 13:31-32).

Little become much when God is in it!

The Boy's Lunch

Oh, how I would have loved to have been in the crowd of people who gathered on a hillside near the Sea of Galilee to hear Jesus speak.

When He saw the multitude, Jesus asked Phillip, *"Where shall we buy bread for these people to eat?* (John 6:5).

Jesus was only testing Phillip because He already knew what He was about to do.

Then Phillip answered Him, *"Eight months' wages would not buy enough bread for each one to have a bite!"* (v.7).

One of the disciples, Andrew, spoke up and told the Lord, *"Here is a boy with five small barley loaves and two small fish, but how far will they go among so many?"*(v.9)

Jesus had the people sit down on the ground—there were about 5,000 in the crowd. Then He took the loaves, gave thanks and *"distributed to those who were seated as much as they wanted. He did the same with the fish"* (v.11).

When everyone had eaten their fill, He said to His disciples, *"Gather the pieces that are left over. Let nothing be wasted"* (v.12).

So they collected the leftovers and there were twelve basketfuls! What a multiplying Master!

Are Tithes Seed?

After speaking on the subject of seed planting and God's principles of increase, a man walked up to me and said, "Well, I guess I don't have to worry. I've been a tithe payer all of my life."

He was rather surprised when I replied,

> **"Sir, your tithe is not your seed. That's not what the Lord multiplies. The first ten percent already belongs to God—it isn't yours in the first place."**

I hope you understand that in financial terms, your seed comes out of *your* ninety percent. Why? Because it represents your decision, not God's. It is your *offering* that becomes seed.

It's Robbery!

You may be shocked to learn that according to the Barna Research Group only eight percent of those in the United States who call themselves born again Christians pay tithes. Here's another way to look at it. The remaining ninety-two percent may try to sow seed but the Lord doesn't receive it because they haven't tithed.

God asks this question, *"Will a man rob God? Yet you rob me. But you ask, 'How do we rob you?' In tithes and offerings. You are under a curse – the whole nation of you – because you are robbing me"* (Malachi 3:8-9).

The Almighty is saying,

"I can't receive your offering if you've not given a tithe – because the tithe is holy unto Me. If you have not honored Me, you are cursed with a curse."

Friend, how can God bless what He has cursed? I think it's time for believers to take an introspective look at their covenant with the Lord—and His requirements for blessings.

Productive and Increasing

Recently, I took an inventory of my life and found the fruit from the seed I have been planting year after year is now maturing. It has reached such growth that a harvest is now coming from every direction—in my family, my relationships, my ministry and our church.

At this stage of my life it seems that everything is both productive and increasing.

When I travel to conferences and crusades, I pray, "Lord, help me leave the people with enough seed so they will also have a perpetual harvest."

Activate It!

How can your seed propagate and multiply if it dies before it ever has a chance to live?

If I place a seed in the palm of your hand and it stays there tightly gripped for 24 hours, I can almost guarantee it will begin to decay. It soon becomes nonproductive and begins to rot like old manna.

But if you are willing to activate what God has given, it not only lives, but thrives!

Your role may not be "up front" or behind a pulpit, yet it is just as vital.

Do you realize there are certain people across the world who are on their knees praying every time Billy Graham walks on the platform to preach the Gospel? That's their calling—their ministry.

When the rewards are presented in heaven, those prayer warriors will stand shoulder to shoulder with the heralded evangelist. They will each share the blessing for the millions who came to Christ because of their efforts.

Jesus tells us, *"whoever wants to become great among you must be your servant, and whoever wants to be first must be slave of all. For even the Son of Man did not come to be served, but to serve, and to give his life as a ransom for many"* (Mark 10:43-45).

Servanthood and seed planting are inseparably linked.

What Does it Represent?

It's not the size of the seed but its significance that matters. What does it represent when compared to the totality of your life? What has it *cost* you? How much time, commitment, prayer and effort has gone into what you are sowing?

Go ahead and start planting – knowing that in the kernel of every seed lies an incredible abundance just waiting to be released.

Speak these words to the Lord:

As I sow my seed of significance, I must sow:

- In Faith—this declares what I *believe.*
- In Expectancy (Hope)— this declares what I *see.*
- In Obedience—this declares whom I *serve.*

My declaration is that this is my year, my time to transition from just being a giver to being a ***Significant Seed Sower.***

This is my year of blessing!

CHAPTER 8

REAPING IN A FAMINE

How would you react if your father died, your investments failed and your family was facing starvation?

That's the dilemma Isaac was forced to contend with following the death of Abraham. The Bible records *"there was a famine in the land"* (Genesis 26:1) and the people were fleeing to Egypt as they had done in previous times of drought.

The Lord, however, had different plans for Isaac. He gave this directive, *"Do not go down to Egypt; live in the land where I tell you to live. Stay in this land for a while, and I will be with you and will bless you. For to you and your descendants I will give all these lands and will confirm the oath I swore to your father Abraham"* (Genesis 26:2-3).

In the midst of this bleak future, the Lord said, "Isaac, not only do I want you to stay where you are, I desire that you take the seed you possess and begin to sow."

I can visualize Isaac questioning, "Wait a minute,

Lord. It's one thing to remain in this barren land, yet another to realize this is the only seed I have—this is all my father left me!"

God replied, "I know this is true, but I am commanding you to release it."

Scripture tells us, *"Then Isaac sowed in that land"* (Genesis 26:12 KJV).

The Promise

Think of it! The soil was a farmer's nightmare and wouldn't produce for anyone, yet Isaac was faithful and planted because God told him to!

Of course, he hesitated, wanting to hold onto what he had, but the Lord commanded, "Give it!"

Isaac acted in obedience. Why? Because God had given the same promise to him that He made to his father, Abraham, *"I will make your descendants as numerous as the stars in the sky and will give them all these lands, and through your offspring all nations on earth will be blessed, because Abraham obeyed me and kept my requirements, my commands, my decrees and my laws"* (Genesis 26:4-5).

How could Isaac refuse to obey the Lord who had made such a pledge?

Isaac refused to look at the circumstances or follow the parade of others who fled. He realized there was a special calling on his life that must be fulfilled.

What Made the Difference?

What a dynamic lesson for us today! We can't sow our seed based on someone else's experience—whether or not they have been blessed. We must start planting because God tells us to!

Isaac tilled the soil on the same land where crops had miserably failed, yet he was about to receive a great reward? What made the difference?

He had a guarantee from Heaven— something the others didn't possess!

Not only did Isaac sow in that land, the Bible says, *"and the same year [he] reaped a hundred fold because the Lord blessed him"* (Genesis 26:12).

That almost boggles the mind! A hundred fold increase in the "same year"—the year of the famine. Meanwhile, everyone else was starving.

I can imagine Isaac hiring security guards to protect his harvest since he was the only one reaping an abundance.

For Isaac, the blessings were just beginning. Scripture tells us, *"The man became rich, and his wealth continued to grow until he became very wealthy. He had so many flocks and herds and servants that the Philistines envied him"* (vv.13-14).

"You're an Heir!"

Why is this story so relevant for you and me?

We have something the world doesn't possess—a vow from the Almighty that insures a glorious future.

Even more, because we have accepted Christ, God's nature is within us.

Friend, the same covenant God made with Abraham and Isaac is ours! Remember, *"If you belong to Christ, then you are Abraham's seed, and heirs according to the promise"* (Galatians 3:29).

We need to grasp the significance of what God told Isaac.

The Lord was telling him—and also us: "I am about to do something in your life based on the promise I made to your father. And since you are his heir, that same vow is also yours!"

Praise the Lord!

A Fresh Start

Like Isaac, we have an awesome heritage.

In the midst of a corrupt world, the Lord called out a man named Noah. He was *"a righteous man, blameless among the people of his time, and he walked with God"* (Genesis 6:9).

The Lord ordered him to build an ark which made him a laughingstock since there had been no rain. Yet, when God opened the skies and water drenched the earth, Noah, his family, plus two of all living creatures were spared.

When the great flood subsided, God told Noah, *"Come out of the ark, you and your wife and your sons and their wives. Bring out every kind of living creature that is with you – the birds, the animals, and all the creatures that move along the ground – so they can multiply on the earth and be fruitful and increase in number upon it"* (Genesis 8:16-17).

Immediately after they walked on dry ground and built an altar of thanksgiving, God declared the immutable law of seedtime and harvest for *"as long as the earth endures"* (v.22).

**It was time for a new beginning.
After the world had been cleansed, God told
Noah exactly how to sow the right seed.**

"We're Getting Old!"

Genesis 11 traces the lineage from one of Noah's sons,

Shem, to Abraham who was told, *"Unto thy seed will I give this land"* (Genesis 12:7 KJV). God promised he would be the father of a great nation.

Yet, there were serious lessons Abraham needed to learn concerning *where* and *how* to sow.

Again and again, the Lord assured this chosen leader that his descendants would form a mighty nation. But *what* descendants? Abraham and Sarah were growing old with no children in sight.

> *Here was a man in his nineties, with a wife ten years younger—living with the belief that God was going to give them a child.*

Desperate for an answer, Sarah brought her Egyptian handmaiden, Hagar, to Abraham and said, "She is my possession and I want to give her to you. Go ahead and sleep with her, and if you produce a child it will be just like mine"—since slaves were considered property. She added, *"...perhaps I can build a family through her"* (Genesis 16:2).

Even though it was wrong, Abraham did what he was asked to do by his wife. He slept with Hagar and she conceived.

The Wrong Advice

Today, I repeatedly meet those who have been pressured into behavior they know in their heart is not right. Yet, in their desire to please people, they compromise their integrity and values. The results are often tragic.

It happened to Abraham.

By listening to the wrong advice,
he sowed into ground God never meant
for him to touch—planting his seed
where it shouldn't be.

After Hagar became pregnant, Sarah began to despise the woman—mistreating her to such an extent the Egyptian maidservant fled into the desert. An angel stopped her, saying, *"Go back to your mistress and submit to her."* (Genesis 16:9). And the angel added, *"I will so increase your descendants that they will be too numerous to count"* (v.10).

Unfortunately, this was not the seed Abraham was to sow for blessing. The son born to this out-of-wedlock union was Ishmael, about whom the angel prophesied, *"He will be a wild donkey of a man; his hand will be against everyone and everyone's hand against him, and he will live in hostility toward all his brothers"* (v.12).

Two Sons

Biblical scholars trace the present conflicts in the Middle East back to the birth of Ishmael whose descendants populated the Arab world.

I believe the global turmoil we are seeing is a direct result of Abraham's sin. Yet, God gave him a second chance when the angel of the Lord told him, "Listen, you know what the Lord promised. You are going to have a child – she will become pregnant."

It sounded impossible that a 100-year-old man and a 90-year-old woman would become parents. Yet it happened, and Isaac was born.

Sarah smiled, *"God has brought me laughter, and everyone who hears about this will laugh with me"* (Genesis 21:6). And she added, *"Who would have said to Abraham that Sarah would nurse children? Yet I have borne him a son in his old age"* (v.7).

God honored His Word, and now there were two sons in the picture. However, the Lord assured Abraham that it would be *"through Isaac that your offspring will be reckoned"* (v.12).

But what about Ishmael? What would happen to his seed? The Lord declared, *"I will make the son of the maidservant into a nation also, because he is your offspring"* (v.13).

*Two sons—two distinct nations. Every
seed produces after its own kind!*

The Scarlet Cord

From Noah to Abraham, Isaac and even today, when
God makes a promise, it is accompanied by a command
that we participate in His plan. In other words, we must
act on what He says.

For example, the Lord promised Joshua he would
conquer Jericho, but it required the participation of a
prostitute named Rahab who put out a scarlet cord in her
window to signal the armies of Israel (Joshua 2:17-18). It
also represents the fact that she had been cleansed – and
became part of the bloodline of Christ (Matthew 1:5).

Seed for Nineveh

Remember Jonah? We know the story of how he was
told by God to sail for Nineveh and preach to that sinful
city. Instead, he ran from God and was swallowed by a
giant fish.

Repentant, Jonah asked the Lord to deliver him, yet
God still required this wayward servant to sow the
message of deliverance into the city of Nineveh.

Jonah came out preaching because he fully understood

95

that if he didn't plant the seed he would be doomed.

Etched in the heart of God is the fact nothing will ever come forth without the law of seedtime and harvest being demonstrated.

A New Beginning

In the New Testament we read the marvelous story of how God gave man a fresh start by planting His seed in the womb of Mary so a Savior would come to earth. It has resulted in a harvest of countless souls for the Kingdom.

All of God's promises are part of His law of seedtime and harvest. He vowed to send a Messiah who would save the people from their sins—and He fulfilled that pledge. "For God so loved the world that He gave His only begotten son"—this is His seed. That "whosoever believeth in Him shall not perish, but have everlasting life" – this is how His seed comes alive!

If the Creator could not initiate a new beginning without a seed, what makes us think we can?

Your Second Chance

Like Abraham and Jonah, you may have made terrible

mistakes along the way, but a loving God is waiting to give you a second chance. Are you wiling to return to the vision the Lord has revealed? If you are, He will restore your passion and purpose—causing that original seed to grow into His promise for your destiny.

Praise God—your days of famine are over!

CHAPTER 9

DECLARE IT!

The timeless principles of sowing and reaping deposited throughout God's Word suddenly come alive when we make a commitment to act upon them.

As you have been reading these chapters, perhaps you have said to yourself, "This is a good thought," or "I agree with that." But what impact will it have on your life tomorrow, next week or next year?

Today, take a bold step of faith and make a personal decision to incorporate these truths into your daily living. I am asking you to do more than simply read the following ten declarations—I want you to speak them out loud so they will come alive. Make them yours!

Declaration #1:
I already possess an abundance in the form of a seed.

How incredible when we stop to think that God created each of His children with unique gifts. Most people, however, fail to realize these are actual living *seeds* filled with potential. The ability to sing, to teach or to lead is not universal—what the Lord has placed within you is specifically yours and you are expected to plant and nurture that seed.

Paul the apostle says, *"We have different gifts, according to the grace given us. If a man's gift is prophesying, let him use it in proportion to his faith. If it is serving, let him serve; if it is teaching, let him teach; if it is encouraging, let him encourage; if it is contributing to the needs of others, let him give generously; if it is leadership, let him govern diligently; if it is showing mercy, let him do it cheerfully"* (Romans 12:6-8).

The pattern is clear.

Our gift is not to be hidden for safekeeping, rather to be released so it will touch the lives of others.

I constantly meet those who strive to make a name for themselves through imitation—being someone they are not. Instead, they need to pause for a moment and realize they already *possess* the ingredients for achievement. It came to them in the form of a seed which has the power to open incredible doors. As

King Solomon wrote, *"A man's gift maketh room for him, and bringeth him before great men"* (Proverbs 18:16 KJV).

It is God's gift, not yours, that produces the harvest.

Declaration #2:

My supply for tomorrow starts with whatever is in my hand today.

A salesman once told me, "In order to sign one contract I need to make presentations to seven people." He was putting into practice a basic law that requires sowing significant seed today for tomorrow's harvest.

I hear people talking "pie in the sky" concerning the future, ignorant of the fact that what they are doing *now* will determine their dream. Today's small investment eventually yields substantial dividends.

This same law affects our spiritual walk. We're so anxious to receive God's instant blessing that we pray at noon and expect an answer by one o'clock—upset when it doesn't arrive!

Take another look at the parable of the sower (Mark 4:6) and you'll understand there is an interim period between planting and reaping.

The reason so many find themselves in dire straits

—both materially and spiritually—is because of the yesterdays they have allowed to slip by.

Friend, it is not too late to start sowing. It's the only way to guarantee an abundant future.

Declaration #3:

Every seed I possess has the ability to multiply if I sow it in fertile soil.

I've been asked, "Pastor, how can I determine the best place to give?"

There's only one way to evaluate what is "good ground." It's where God *tells* you to sow.

You can't make wise decisions based solely on circumstances or outward appearances. Just because an organization appears needy or someone "looks poor" should not be the measuring stick for your gift. Keep faithfully praying and asking the Lord, "Please guide my giving decisions."

If God gives the okay and you feel at peace, that's all you need; you're sowing in good ground.

You are not acting alone. It is the Lord who

produces the harvest through the seed He has asked you to sow. In reality, this lifts the pressure from your shoulders. When God ordains and selects the soil, He makes certain what is planted will be ready for reaping.

Declaration #4:
God will never know I truly desire a harvest until I sow a seed.

You demonstrate to the Lord what you are believing for in your life the instant you begin to plant. For example:

- God knows you want someone to pray for you when you begin to pray for others.
- The Lord recognizes your longing for friends when you become friendly.
- Your Heavenly Father knows you are ready for a blessing when you pay your tithe and give for the Gospel's sake.

We set our standards by the manner in which we sow our seed.

When I'm driving in heavy traffic and see a car trying to enter the street, if at all possible, I let the vehicle in. Why? Because I know there will be a time when I will expect the same courtesy.

Perhaps you are believing God for a healing. Ask yourself, "How many sick people have I prayed for today?"

While attending a board meeting of a Christian organization, I noticed an older gentleman who always seemed to be by himself—he was conspicuously alone. He looked beaten down both emotionally and physically and my heart went out to him.

One afternoon, while taking a shuttle bus back to our hotel, I intentionally sat next to this man and, happy for my interest, he began to share his story. Apparently, because of a church board which became upset when he attempted to follow the Lord's leading, this once-mighty man of God was forced to leave his beloved congregation. Now, at the age of 65, he had just started a new church.

Despite the new beginning, he was still harboring bitterness and despondency over what had transpired during the previous five years.

Instantly, the Lord directed me to pour love and encouragement into this dear pastor during the next couple of days. We began talking enthusiastically about the future, not dwelling on the past— becoming excited about what God was about to accomplish in his current ministry.

_____ ❦ _____

*Before we left the meeting, he had
a radiant smile on his face, a new vision
and renewed strength.*

What caused the turn-around? Someone had sown into his life.

That isn't the end of the story. Not long after that experience, there entered a challenge in my own life and God graciously sent an individual to help me carry the burden. It was as if the Lord was reassuring me, saying, "You've sown your seed, now get ready to reap!"

Declaration #5:

My seed cannot release it's potential until I let go of it.

Have you ever gone out of your way to be nice to a person, only to be treated rudely? Our natural human reaction is to feel slighted and say, "Well, I don't have to put up with this!"

If that's our response, we have just dug up our seed!

God asks us to plant with a pure heart—and leave it there.

When you are given a cold shoulder, smile and continue to love that individual in spite of their attitude.

You are not looking for a plaque on your wall or a "Man of the Year" award. What you are doing is unto the Lord—not for self. That's why you must totally release your seed, and regardless of the circumstances, never attempt to retrieve it.

Because this is so important, let me remind you once more: when you sow into the lives of others, never expect them to give you a harvest. They are not your source—God is! If they *never* respond, that is not the issue. The potential can only be realized by you releasing the seed.

Let go and let God!

Declaration #6:

For every need I may encounter, God has a seed to meet my need.

Men and women have come to my office to unburden their hearts, saying, "Pastor, you don't understand what I am going through!"

That's a true statement:

- I cannot identify with a guy whose life is nearly ruined from long term drug abuse.
- I cannot identify with the individual who was taken advantage of in business and lost everything he owned.
- I cannot identify with a wife whose husband just brutally beat her.
- I cannot identify with a person who has lost his family through divorce.

Oh, I can have deep compassion, empathy, and love them, yet my feet have not walked in their shoes.

What I do know is this: whatever need a person has, whether large or small, God has the required seed.

To the alcoholic, the seed may be a 12-step recovery program. To the lonely and depressed, it may be a circle of caring Christian friends. To the person sinking into bankruptcy, it may be a new opportunity to make a fresh start.

The Lord can give you seeds of creativity, vision, motivation and determination. Your task is to discover exactly what God desires for you to sow.

This is not some magical, mystical process. It is fervently praying until God reveals His perfect will for you—then stepping out in faith!

Declaration #7:

I accept the fact that seed time and harvest is not necessarily comfortable.

Sowing and reaping is not based on facts, logic and reasoning. Rather, it is God's eternal law.

As a result, the Lord stretches and expands our faith and removes us from our comfort zone to accomplish His purpose.

For example, it's tough to hear God whisper, "Sow the seed you possess," when you are down to your last dollar. And it is difficult to pray for a neighbor who is sick when a member of your own family is suffering with a life-threatening illness.

However, seedtime and harvest is not based upon you being comfortable.

Paul writes, *"But I keep under my body, and bring it into subjection: lest that by any means, when I have preached to others, I myself should be a castaway"* (1 Corinthians 9:27 KJV).

The apostle knew that following God's mandate meant he needed self-discipline—to keep himself constrained so he would not be *body*-ruled, but *spirit* ruled.

I've encountered those who refuse to obey when the Holy Spirit directs them. Instead they waste their potential on something trivial, not realizing the only way that particular seed could change their circumstances is if it were *sown*.

Others make statements which destroy their harvest for tomorrow. They have not learned to bring themselves under subjection—to bite their lip and be tolerant when those around them are abrasive.

Personally, my actions are not based upon what somebody else has done, rather I seek to demonstrate kindness because it is a fruit of the Spirit. And I don't give according to the amount of money I may have in the bank, rather in response to what the Holy Spirit has directed me to give.

As I'm sure you have learned, it is not always easy.

Declaration #8:

If I am committed to be a sower, the Lord will provide the seed.

Some believers have the mistaken impression that when they sow they must permanently sacrifice or do without until their time of harvest arrives.

Wrong! God promises to sustain those who plant during the time it takes their seed to multiply. *"Now he who supplies seed to the sower and bread for food will also supply and increase your store of seed and He will enlarge the harvest of your righteousness"* (2 Corinthians 9:10).

God always keeps His promises!

We need to realize Satan cannot destroy our harvest – only we can!

Let me tell you why.

When I bring my tithe, I am declaring God is the Most High God, the possessor of heaven and earth. Therefore, I have taken that which is in the natural and moved it into the spiritual by declaring what belongs to the Lord—and Satan cannot steal what is God's. That is why the Almighty says, *"I will rebuke the devourer for your sakes"* (Malachi 3:11 KJV). This is because what you give has been removed from your hand—and the devil cannot prevent God's blessings from being poured out. Why? Because your offering establishes the size of your outpouring.

Satan is limited to only sowing weeds in our harvest field. Jesus speaks concerning this when He compares the kingdom of heaven to *"a man who sowed good seed in his field. But while everyone was sleeping, his enemy came and sowed weeds among the wheat, and went away"* (Matthew 13:24-25).

Of course, the unwanted weeds sprouted along

with the wheat. Then the owner's servants came and asked, *"Do you want us to pull them up?"* (v.28).

"No," he answered, *"because while you are pulling the weeds, you may root up the wheat with them. Let both grow together until the harvest"* (Matthew 13:29-30).

There are church members who bring their tithes and offerings to the sanctuary, yet if an event happens in the congregation they don't like, they take offense, become emotional and want to tear things up—blind to the fact they are pulling up their potential harvest at the same time. Satan doesn't cause the chaos, we do!

Our crop, including those pesky weeds, must keep growing until the final reaping.

Declaration #9:
God is aware of my need.

I smile when I hear people complain, "Pastor, God is going to take everything away from me!"

Well, if that was the Lord's intention, He would already have it!

My friend, God is totally cognizant of exactly what you require and when you need His assistance. It's not His will that you suffer while you are fulfilling His promise.

Do you remember Job? It wasn't the Lord who instigated his problems. Instead, to test Job's faith, God *allowed* Satan to try him. The Lord is not a vengeful Father who looks for opportunities to punish His children. No, He wants to make us mighty and strong.

God doesn't ask you to sow just for the experience. It's what He expects as your permanent lifestyle—based on His laws of planting and reaping, giving and receiving.

In the process, like every good Father, He is carefully watching over His own.

Declaration #10:

The seed that I sow may be for the need of another, yet it is also for my harvest.

We can't escape God's law that declares, *"Give, and it will be given to you"* (Luke 6:38).

The moment you begin to plant your seed to meet a need, a glorious process commences. Not only will it bless the life of the recipient, you will benefit too. It's like a boomerang! Jesus tells you, *"For with the measure you use, it will be measured to you"* (Luke v.38).

Perhaps it's time to ask yourself, "What is the size of the harvest I am looking for? Is it one that will only require a small container? Or am I ready to reap an *overflowing* reward?"

Finally, you must determine the depth of your commitment. What price are you willing to pay to see the Lord begin to move in your finances, your relationships and your spiritual growth?

Remember this: *"Whoever sows sparingly will also reap sparingly, and whoever sows generously will also reap generously"* (2 Corinthians 9:6).

Declare it and start sowing!

CHAPTER 10

IS YOUR SEED SIGNIFICANT?

There are those who spend a lifetime playing "Trivial Pursuit." They happily settle for average, and as long as they somehow scrape by, nothing else really matters.

The same attitude seeps into their spiritual life—being a mediocre Christian who rarely prays, never witnesses to their neighbors and would much rather watch a rerun of "The Jeffersons" for the tenth time than make it to church on Sunday night.

Paul talks about such people when he writes, *"Some have wandered away from [a sincere faith] and turned to meaningless talk"* (1 Timothy 1:6).

What's the Value?

When I first began sharing the concept of "significant seed," there were more than a few who thought I was talking only about the *quantity* of what was being planted. While it is true God desires that we sow generously, He is more concerned for our seed to be meaningful—representing true significance.

We need to continually ask ourselves, "Does what I spend my time on have real value?"

Of course, we must be compassionate with those who ask for our help, yet that does not mean we must waste countless hours with them in idle conversation. Is it really necessary to be constantly on the phone listening to gossip, complaining and rehashing old topics?

There comes a time when we must draw a line and step into a new beginning—to embrace those things which have true significance.

A Profitable God

I've heard preachers lash out against a checklist of "sins" people should abandon. However, there is another vice God desires that we give up which we seldom hear about. What is it? That which is meaningless and makes no positive contribution to our future.

It's vital to understand the Lord does nothing in your life that is not profitable.

Jesus focused on this fact when He shared the Parable of the Talents. He told the story of a man who was about to go on a journey. Before leaving, the landowner called his three servants together and entrusted his property to them.

To one he gave five talents, to another he gave two, and the third was given one talent. A "talent" represented more than $1,000.

What is fascinating about this parable is that the master gave to each *"according to his ability"* (Matthew 25:15). In other words, he gave them only what he thought they could handle.

When the master returned from his long absence, the Bible says he *"reckoneth with them"* (v.19 KJV). Reckoning is an accounting term describing a check of the records to determine profit or loss.

The landowner looked at the books and saw that the servants to whom he had entrusted the five and two talents had each doubled his money through wise investments.

He congratulated them for being profitable servants.

However, the man who received only one talent was fearful and afraid. He buried his money and had only the original amount left to return.

The master chastised him as a *"wicked, lazy servant"* (v.26). Even more, he took the talent from the man and gave it to the one who had produced ten talents!

What was the difference between the three servants? The first two did something significant with the funds with which they had been given. They made meaningful investments.

Pruning Time!

The Lord is searching for those who have a commitment to *produce*.

Jesus once described Himself as a vine, with His Father as the gardener (John 15:1). And what does the Almighty do to increase the harvest? *"He cuts off every branch in me that bears no fruit, while every branch that does bear fruit he prunes so that it will be even more fruitful"* (v.2).

Since Christ is the vine and we are the branches, if we remain *attached* to Him, we will *"bear much fruit" [because] apart from me you can do nothing"* (v.5).

However, *"If anyone does not remain in me, he is like a branch that is thrown away and withers; such branches are picked up, thrown into the fire and burned"* (v.6).

The Lord intends that we produce—and *remain* productive.

Producing and Reproducing

In Genesis 1, God spoke ten times—and in each

instance the Bible says, "He created...He created...He created.

Then, whether it be trees, flowers, creatures of the sea, animals or birds, He gave them the responsibility of reproducing themselves. *"The land produced vegetation: plants bearing seed according to their kinds"* (Genesis 1: 12). God said, *"Let the land produce living creatures according to their kinds"* (v.24).

When it came to the first man and woman whom the Almighty created in His likeness (v.26), there was one additional command. Not only are we to multiply on the earth (be productive), we are to "rule" or "have dominion" over everything God created (exercise authority).

Here's the sequence. *First* we are to be productive; *then* we come into authority.

Bold Action

The Bible tells us the Word of God was given not only that we be chastened and corrected, but so we might profit from studying its inspired pages.

As Paul wrote to young Timothy, *"All scripture is given by inspiration of God, and is profitable for doctrine, for reproof, for correction, for instruction in righteousness"* (2 Timothy 3:16 KJV).

It's the *significant* seed—with meaning and value—which becomes fruitful.

The person who is armed with the Word and ready for a spiritual transformation needs to take bold action. They can't continue to repeat the same old patterns in the same old ways!

As a pastor, I have noticed that when certain people truly need a touch from God, their behavior changes. Instead of sitting quietly in the sanctuary, suddenly their hands are lifted in worship and their voices are raised in praise. I believe they attract God's attention by the sincerity of their actions.

Meaningful seed is profitable—and produces change.

THE FOUR QUALITIES OF SIGNIFICANT SEED

What you sow may seem minuscule, yet it has incredible potential to impact every corner of your life. Let's examine these profound qualities:

1. Your seed has *spiritual* significance.

There's an eternal difference between what is sown by man or planted by God. As a believer, you have tapped into seed which touches your spirit—and will never die.

The apostle Peter declares, *"For you have been born again, not of perishable seed, but of imperishable, through the living and enduring word of God"* (1 Peter 1:23).

Not only has our heart been cleansed through the precious blood of Jesus, we have been given God's Word which has a miraculous power to multiply. We know that the sower *"sows the word"* (Mark 4:14) and it has the ability to produce a great harvest.

The potential for a remarkable time of reaping is directly related to how we receive the Word.

Jesus says, some, *"like seed sown among thorns, hear the word, but the worries of this life, the deceitfulness of wealth and the desire for other things come in and choke the word, making it unfruitful"* (vv.18-19).

What a difference when we cherish and honor the Word, *"Others, like seed sown on good soil, hear the word, accept it, and produce a crop—thirty, sixty or even a hundred times what was sown"* (v.20).

Spiritual matters require spiritual seed—and that's why God's written Word is essential for our growth.

2. Your seed has *soul* significance

The "soulish" realm encompasses our mind and emotions—which cause us to be affected by circumstances or moved by the moment.

Scripture tells us there is both spiritual knowledge (revelation insight) and carnal knowledge (the education of the world).

We can learn our ABC's, math and history through reading and studying, but spiritual understanding is only released when we allow God's seed to be sown within us.

This is why Paul declares, *"Do not conform any longer to the pattern of this world, but be transformed by the renewing of your mind. Then you will be able to test and approve what God' will is—his good, pleasing and perfect will"* (Romans 12:2).

Later, the apostle tells us to take control of our thoughts—to focus on what is true, honest, just, pure and lovely. He says, *"...whatsoever things are of good report; if there be any virtue, and if there be any praise, think on these things"* (Philippians 4:8 KJV).

To have the mind of God, we need a *renovation* of our thought process. The Bible declares, *"You were taught, with regard to your former way of life, to put off your old self, which is being corrupted by its deceitful desires; to be made new in the attitude of your minds; and to put on the new self, created to be like God in true righteousness and holiness"* (Ephesians 4:22-24).

Without being awake and alert, we will allow the world's system to blindly program our emotions and our mental computers. James tells us, *"Do not merely listen to the word, and deceive yourselves. Do what it says"* (James 1:22).

Our *soulish* realm requires a seed to be sown. The person who witnesses and helps to rescue *"the sinner from the error of his way shall save a soul from death"* (James 5:20 KJV).

Once you have accepted God's Son, you cannot spiritually develop and mature and have the *"mind of Christ"* (1 Corinthians 2:16 KJV) until the Word is firmly embedded within. That's how our soul is renewed.

3. Your seed has *physical* significance.

I can tell you from personal experience if you neglect your body, sooner or later you will pay a high price. Because I was not taking care of myself physically, I suffered a heart attack. Neither God nor Satan was responsible—I did it to myself!

Since that dramatic wake-up call, I have made drastic changes in my eating and exercise habits. After all, my flesh and blood must be a testimony to the God who created me.

We need to say with the psalmist, *"I praise you because I am fearfully and wonderfully made"* (Psalms 139:14).

The person who deliberately allows his or her mortal body to deteriorate ignores God's desire. Paul writes, *"Do you not know that your body is a temple of the Holy Spirit, who is in you, whom you have received from God? You are not your own; you were bought at a price. Therefore honor God with your body"* (1 Corinthians 6:19-20).

> *Your body is a gift from God—and how you treat this "earthen treasure" tells Him how you value that present.*

4. Your seed has *material* significance.

According to the Word, God's principles apply to every facet of our life—not just spirit, soul and body, it also includes our finances. For that reason I never hesitate to claim His promises of material and financial blessings.

It is God's intention for His people to live in abundance—and when they do, He rejoices. King David says, *"Let the Lord be magnified, which hath pleasure in the prosperity of his servant"* (Psalms 35:27 KJV).

How we thrive and flourish, however, is the direct result of following the laws and precepts God has established. For example, what we receive depends on what we invest. Scripture makes it clear that *"If a man will not work, he shall not eat"* (2 Thessalonians 3:10).

You can place yourself in the flow of God's material blessing by establishing a rhythm of giving and receiving, sowing and reaping.

Your Decision

To experience a profound change in your life, start planting in the four fields we've been discussing.

- Forget the past and start investing in your spiritual future.
- Revolutionize your thought-life and feed your soul by diligently seeking the mind of Christ.
- Start treating you body as the temple of the Holy Spirit it truly is.
- Change your economic future by becoming a giver rather than a taker.

Don't spend another day floundering in the valley of indecision. God will help transform your future when you start sowing significant seed.

CHAPTER 11

A NEVER-ENDING HARVEST

The potential of a minute seed is mind-boggling. However, when it is sown in the field of faith—and according to God's laws—the results are even more miraculous.

Your significant seed doesn't only produce enough to sustain you for a month or a year. It results in a *perpetual* harvest, one that continues to bless you for eternity.

God's Word proves it!

Here's the Evidence!

When Abraham was well over 100 years old, God spoke to him concerning a requirement he was to fulfill. Scripture tells us *"that God did tempt Abraham"* (Genesis 22:1 KJV).

Don't let the word "tempt" throw you off track. In the original Hebrew the meaning is "prove." After all, the Bible says, *"God cannot be tempted...nor does he tempt anyone*" (James 1:13).

To *tempt* means, "I don't know what you will or will not do, so let's put you to the test." To *prove*, however, says, "I going to bring evidence to the table which shows what is already in place." That's what the Lord was about to do with Abraham.

Why would Jehovah want to *prove* something to him? Because here was the man through whom God declared all the nations of the world would be blessed.

In the life of Abraham, the Almighty was setting in motion a series of events which would result in the greatest seed ever to be sown—His Son, Jesus.

A Permanent Message

God wasn't just proving Himself to Abraham, He was establishing something in the heavenlies. What was about to take place would send a permanent message to Lucifer, the fallen angel, and all of his demons.

A voice from heaven spoke directly to Abraham: "*Take your son, your only son, Isaac, whom you love, and go to the region of Moriah. Sacrifice him there as a burnt offering on one of the mountains I will tell you about*" (Genesis 22:2).

As the Bible records, early the next morning, Abraham

rose up and saddled his donkey. He took with him two of his servants and his son, Isaac. First, he cut up enough wood for the burnt offering and then headed for the place God had instructed him to go.

On the third day, *"Abraham looked up and saw the place in the distance. He said to his servants, 'Stay here with the donkey while I and the boy go over there. We will worship and then we will come back to you'"* (vv.4-5).

Following God's orders, Abraham took the wood for the burnt offering and gave it to Isaac to carry, while he himself held the flint (the fire) and the knife.

The Ultimate Request

What a time of inner-turmoil this must have been for Abraham. God was saying, "I want you to offer your son to me as a sacrifice. I am placing a demand on you to give up what is most precious in your life—what you value more than anything else."

In essence, the Almighty was telling Abraham, "There will be nothing between you and Me. Give Me your son."

Without question, Isaac was a significant, meaningful seed.

As the father and son walked together, Isaac turned to Abraham and said, *"The fire and wood are here...but where is the lamb for the burnt offering"* (v. 7). Abraham answered, *"God himself will provide the lamb"* (v.8), and they continued their journey.

"Don't Worry, Isaac"

You may say, "I thought God told Abraham that *Isaac* would be the sacrifice."

Let's look at how this event was recorded in the book of Hebrews: *"By faith Abraham, when God tested him, offered Isaac as a sacrifice. He who had received the promises was about to sacrifice his one and only son, even though God had said to him, 'It is through Isaac that your offspring will be reckoned.' Abraham reasoned that God could raise the dead, and figuratively speaking, he did receive Isaac back from death"* (Hebrews 11:17-19).

This tells us God is going to provide because He *always* gives seed to the sower. It is why Abraham could tell his son, "Don't worry, Isaac, God is going to supply a lamb."

I believe Abraham told Isaac, "Regardless of what happens, you are significant. Trust God and trust me."

When the altar had been prepared, Abraham arranged the wood and bound his son on the sacrifice. *"Then he reached out his hand and took the knife to slay his son"* (Genesis 22:10).

Suddenly, the angel of the Lord called out to him from heaven, "Abraham! Abraham!"

"Here I am," he replied.

The angel said, *"Do not lay a hand on the boy...Do not do anything to him. Now I know that you fear God, because you have not withheld from me your son, your only son"* (v.12).

Abraham looked up and saw behind him a ram caught in the thicket by his horns. The Bible tells how he went over and sacrificed it as a burnt offering instead of Isaac (v.13).

Abraham named the place, "The Lord Will Provide."

It was Forever

Next, the angel called from heaven the second time with an announcement declaring Abraham had not just offered a significant seed, but one which was *perpetual*.

The angel said, *"I swear by myself, declares the Lord, that because you have done this and have not withheld your son, your only son, I will surely bless you and make your descendants as numerous as the stars in the sky and as the sand on the seashore. Your descendants will take possession of the cities of their enemies, and through your offspring all nations on earth will be blessed, because you have obeyed me"* (Genesis 22:16-18).

Praise God, the harvest was *forever!*

Here's how that seed affects you and me today. The apostle Paul writes, *"...for all of you who were baptized into Christ have clothed yourselves with Christ. There is neither Jew nor Greek, slave nor free, male nor female, for you are all one in Christ Jesus. If you belong to Christ, then you are Abraham's seed, and heirs according to the promise"* (Galatians 3:27-29).

It's Your Inheritance

Not only was Isaac a significant, perpetual seed—so are you, and so am I. If we are in Christ, we are heirs according to the promise. Read this passage carefully and you'll realize it is not about religion, culture, politics or whether you are a man or woman. White, black, rich, destitute, educated, uneducated—we all have the same promise.

There's no room for excuses. Forget about past injustices or the circumstances of your upbringing.

What God has planned for your future exceeds any damage of the past.

You complain, "But I wasn't born with a silver spoon in my mouth?"

Neither was I. But one day God began to tell me, "I will make a way where there is no way. I'll give you favor where men cannot find it. I'll open doors that seem to be bolted shut. I will let you share My Word with world leaders."

God fulfilled that promise, not because of my background, but because I walked into my heritage from the perpetual seed of Isaac which Abraham was willing to sow. What I have is an eternal harvest the enemy cannot steal!

A Lifestyle of Giving

I get excited when I think of the potential of significant sowing. However, God has also established that *perpetual giving*—as a lifestyle—produces a *perpetual harvest.*

Many think of the great temple King Solomon built to honor the Lord, and forget it was his father, David, who first had the vision. David gave Solomon, *"the plans of all that the Spirit had put in his mind...for the temple of the Lord"* (1 Chronicles 28:12).

Where did the money come from to build such a magnificent temple? The people gave, and gave and gave—starting with David himself. *"With all my resources I have provided for the temple of my God— gold...silver...bronze"* (1 Chronicles 29:2) as well as precious stones.

Then David challenged the people to do the same. They responded with overwhelming generosity. The Bible records how *"the leaders of families, the officers of the tribes of Israel, the commanders of thousands and commanders of hundreds, and the officials in charge of the king's work gave willingly*" (1 Chronicles 29:6).

We're not talking nickels and dimes. They gave 10,000 talents of silver, 18,000 talents of bronze and 100,000 talents of iron (v.7) Plus, *"Any who had precious stones gave them to the treasury of the temple of the Lord"* (v.8).

A Gift of Love

David, who set the example, still wasn't finished with his giving. The Bible tells us he gave his *"personal treasures of gold and silver for the temple of my God"* (v.3). David was saying, "My affection is continually toward the House of God, so I want to give even more."

This was beyond responding to a need—David was presenting his earthly possessions to the Lord as an act of worship.

What a powerful lesson. Instead of just being "need oriented," we must sow what is *meaningful*. It was David's love for the house of the Lord which led him to give above and beyond what was required.

True Affection

When I married Kathy, I didn't place a ring on her finger because she needed it. If that were the case, I could have gone to a cheap jewelry store and purchased a little band of imitation gold. Instead, I offered her something I was proud of— because it represented my love and affection toward her.

Significance surpasses the ordinary. For example, if you throw a dollar to the fellow on the street corner holding a sign that reads, "Will work for food," you are perpetuating a hand-out lifestyle. But when you make a friend of the individual and bring him to the point where he is willing to really work for a living, you have truly made a significance in his life—transforming him from the past to the future.

Symbolism or Significance?

There is a poignant story in the New Testament of Mary, the sister of Martha and Lazarus coming to Jesus prior to the crucifixion with an alabaster jar of very expensive perfume. The Bible says she *"broke the jar and poured the perfume over his head"* (Mark 14:3).

After she anointed Jesus, some of those present declared indignantly to one another, *"Why this waste of perfume? It could have been sold for more than a year's wages and the money given to the poor"* (Mark 14:4-5). They rebuked Mary harshly.

If we are not careful, we will allow people to talk us out of sowing a seed of significance when we feel compelled to sow it.

They'll comment, "It's crazy! Why would you give money to such a cause?" or "Why would you bless that person?"

Instead of a perpetual harvest, the enemy would rather you have empty fields and no crops.

When the alabaster jar was broken, Jesus said, *"Leave her alone...Why are you bothering her? She has done a beautiful thing to me. The poor you will always have with you, and you can help them any time you want. But you will not always have me. She did what she could. She poured perfume on my body beforehand to prepare for my burial. I tell you the truth, wherever the gospel is preached throughout the world, what she has done will also be told, in memory of her"* (Mark 14:6-9).

The act of this woman was symbolic because she took something priceless and broke it—meaning it could never be used for any other purpose than this. She made the act significant.

It was Jesus who made the seed perpetual—saying, "wherever the gospel is preached, this will be remembered."

What an awesome God we serve!

It has been more than 2000 years since the Father gave His Son to defeat sin in our lives. Yet this seed of significance is still producing a harvest which is perpetually growing and growing.

Are You a "Fruit-Bearer?"

Have you made the decision to release the past and plant a new beginning? Are you ready to sow meaningful seed for an eternal harvest?

The Bible says a *"A good man leaves an inheritance for his children's children"* (Proverbs 13:22). That means he did some significant investing—not just for his kids, but his grandchildren. That's perpetual!

The enemy will use every devise to stop us because he knows the Word tells us we are to *"Be fruitful, and multiply, and replenish the earth"* (Genesis 1:28 KJV). And when that happens, we become people of authority. We take *"dominion over... every living thing that moveth upon the earth"* (v.28).

It's impossible to *replenish* without a perpetual harvest.

The moment you become a "fruit-bearer" you begin to multiply, because God is all about increase and profitability.

As we become involved in harvest after harvest, Satan gets nervous. Why? Because he knows the dreams and visions of a giving person cannot be stopped. The individual who fully understands and participates in the law of the harvest has a destiny which will not be detoured.

Your Everlasting Legacy

When I look at how the Lord has blessed my life and ministry, I realize I am here because of the seed planted by my earthly father and *his* father. Grandpa Thomas built many churches for the Kingdom, and Kathy has the same story. Her parents were faithful in sowing and giving—and her grandparents were involved in the work of the Lord. Before Grandma Burkhard passed from this earth to her heavenly reward, she was helping to support more than twenty ministries around the world.

My children can't *help* but be blessed since the enemy cannot halt what the Lord has started.

Remember, when you are faithful in multiplying, you become a man or woman of authority. The enemy is now beneath your feet. You will be able to declare, *"And God raised us up with Christ and seated us with him in the heavenly realms in Christ Jesus"* (Ephesians 2:6).

Because of what was planted by those who have gone before, I am able to say:

- "Greater is He who is in me, than he who is in the world."
- "I am more than a conqueror through Him who loved me."

■ "I can do all things through Him who strengthens me."

What will be your legacy? What are you planting into the lives of those you love?

Today, Jesus is saying, *"..open your eyes and look at the fields! They are ripe for harvest. Even now the reaper draws his wages, even now he harvests the crop for eternal life"* (John 4:35-36).

It is my prayer that as you sow seeds of significance you will enjoy the abundance of God's perpetual harvest.

NOTES